The Amaz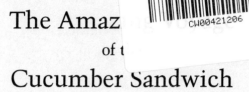
of t
Cucumber Sandwich

The Amazing Voyage

of the

Cucumber Sandwich

A story in three parts,
set in the human body

---

by
Dr Pete Rowan

Illustrated by

Polly Noakes

RIVERSWIFT

LONDON

For my son Edward

Paperback edition first published in
the United Kingdom in 1994 by
Riverswift
Random House, 20 Vauxhall Bridge Road, London SW1V 2SA
A division of Random House UK Ltd
London Melbourne Sydney Auckland Johannesburg
and agencies throughout the world

Random House UK Limited Reg. No. 954009

1 3 5 7 9 10 8 6 4 2

First published by Jonathan Cape Limited 1991

A CIP catalogue record for this book
is available from the British Library

ISBN 1 898304 82 3

Printed and Bound in Great Britain by
Cox & Wyman Ltd, Reading, Berkshire

Contents

Part One

Six African Elephants

This is the story of a fantastic voyage, the intrepid journey of one cucumber sandwich into YOU. All its incredible adventures are here, as it heads towards its final goal.

It is a *true* story, and unless you live a rather unusual life it is highly likely you will eat a cucumber sandwich at some time or other. Perhaps you already have – after all, an average person in the Western world will eat about eleven thousand sandwiches in a lifetime.

If you're lucky enough to live in a part of the world where there is plenty of food the total you will eat during your life is likely to weigh over 30,000 kilograms. This would fill about 750 supermarket trolleys. It's equivalent to the weight of six African elephants. On top of that it's also been worked out that you'll drink about 40,000 litres of fluids. An amazing variety of food makes the journey into you through your open mouth.

But back to sandwiches, the man we have to thank is the fourth Earl of Sandwich, who lived from 1718 to 1792. He was the First Lord of the Admiralty during the American War of Independence. (Although he wasn't much good at the job he had the Sandwich Islands named after him! They're now called Hawaii.) His passion was gambling, which he loved so much that he spent days losing money at the card table. He wouldn't even leave the table to go and eat. (He was a bit like King James I of England, who was so keen on hunting that he wouldn't get off his horse to go to the toilet!)

This single-minded earl used to have hunks of meat brought to him between two pieces of bread, which is how the word sandwich got into the language. (Imagine if they had been named after the Earl of Bath!) The two slices of bread and the variety of food that goes inside can make up a good mixed diet. But you can't possibly work out everything you need in the way of food, so you just have to eat well and let your body get on and sort things out.

One point I should make before this incredible journey begins is that there are bound to be exceptions to some of the amazing facts you'll read here about the human body. There really isn't such a thing as an "average" person. We are all different. If you make any rule there will be an exception to it. One quite good book of crazy facts I have read says man is the only animal that sleeps flat on its back. They have obviously never seen my dog Conker on our best sofa!

Anyway, this book is about the adventures of a sandwich as it travels into you, a journey to show that you really are what you eat.

Down in the Mouth!

The amazing journey begins in your mouth. This is about the only part of the adventure you have complete control over. Until you swallow the cucumber sandwich there's still time to turn back. You can still spit it out. After that, though, your body automatically takes care of it, carrying it down into your innermost parts and turning it into YOU.

All the food you ever eat – the weight of six elephants – has to pass through your mouth. So your mouth is more than just a hole in your face – it's the gateway to the inner you. (It's also useful for speaking and breathing of course!)

The floor of the mouth is taken up by your tongue. The tongue has its root in the back of the mouth, and the front part is mobile. You can stick it out, wiggle it, and use it to speak, to taste or to help mash up the food that the teeth chop up. The roof of the mouth is mainly hard palate – a ceiling of bone which also happens to double up as the floor of your nose.

The teeth are a mixture of shapes, from the sharp incisors at the front which slice the sandwich up, to the flatter-topped molars right at the back which grind

the food. The lips are the junction between the mouth and the outside world. Apart from being useful for speaking and giving signals to other people – such as kissing and smiling – they help keep the food in your mouth while it gets chewed and chopped and sliced up and mixed by the teeth, tongue and muscles of the mouth.

Saliva is added in while this is happening. There are six salivary glands around the mouth, and they pour out saliva when food is about. Seeing and smelling food – or even just thinking about it – sets these glands working. And the more mouth-watering the food is, the more saliva is produced. The watery fluid does a number of things. It liquefies the food so the taste buds can taste it, and it begins the long process of breaking the food down so that the body can take it in. As well as all this, saliva also keeps the mouth clean, and makes speaking easier. Speaking with a very dry mouth is quite difficult.

Once your sandwich is well chewed and the saliva is mixed in, it's ready to go. It's then rolled into a soft ball and positioned in the curve of the tongue. Here it waits for a moment like a large missile in a medieval catapult outside a city under siege. Once swallowing begins, the throat muscles contract and throw the ball back into what is called the pharynx. (You can usually just about see this far if you look down someone's throat.) Once the ball of food hits the back wall of the pharynx things start to happen automatically – it's probably just as well they do as there would be a lot to think about otherwise. Breathing stops for a fraction of a second, the airways to the lungs are blocked off quickly by a flap of tissue like a trap door (the epiglottis), and the gullet (or oesophagus) opens to receive the sandwich and take it down to the stomach. There's certainly no turning back now!

Helter-skelter

The mashed-up sandwich now passes into the gullet, or oesophagus. This is a muscular tube about 25 centimetres long, which squeezes the food down towards the stomach. Even if you were to swallow standing on your head the muscles would propel the food in the right direction.

All this happens without you having to think about it. It's about the fastest part of the journey. The sandwich will be down the helter-skelter in less than the time it takes to read this chapter.

Quite by chance the cucumber sandwich arrives in the stomach on Christmas Day! Inside the body all is dark and warm. Outside it's cold and snow is beginning to fall . . .

Christmas Day in the Stomach: A Diary

25 December

5 a.m. Brain has woken up and given the rest of the body a kick. I've been quiet and empty all night. Spleen's near by and he says I look like a skinny sausage. Liver on the other side agrees.

6.05 a.m. Body just got up and ran downstairs to fridge. Some cold orange juice arrived. Body ran upstairs to parents. Then downstairs again. Very inconsiderate! Tight muscles at my top managed to keep juice down. Body now cartwheeling and tearing off paper from a new bike. Juice still in me.

8.30 a.m. Toast arrived (two rounds) while body was cycling around the garden. (Orange juice disappeared into blood about an hour ago through my walls.) Toast had been badly chewed and was still in great lumps, stuck together with a thick gluey marmalade. I was just churning this up and mixing in various digestive juices when body fell off bike and ran indoors. Tear ducts went berserk. That really threw me. Blood had already moved off to leg muscles to pedal

bike, and then this! My walls have now stopped churning the toast up altogether, and have gone quite pale.

11 a.m. Body feels a bit better. Digestive juices have started to flow again, and I've given a few more squeezes and thumps to the toast. It's beginning to look like a sort of soup. I'm just about to squirt this lot along to duodenum, the next bit of guts. Body is lazing about while brain and eyes watch someone famous on TV wandering around a hospital giving presents to sick children.

12.30 p.m. Our aunt Hilda arrived and kissed cheek. No present again this year from her. This made my walls go red and angry as usual. Mouth swallowed a mince pie. Our mum's pies are very crumbly and light – easy to smash up into bits. I'm passing them on to duodenum fast.

2 p.m. Feeling hungry. Our dad is late back from the pub. I'm gurgling and rumbling by moving about. Body has swallowed a load of air, which is making things worse.

3 p.m. We're off. The big one. A bowl of soup is pouring down gullet. No problem. It won't be long before some of it will be ready to move on.

3.45 p.m.	So far I've received four roast potatoes, a turkey's leg, some chestnut mixture, a pea and carrot mixture, some gravy, and a red sauce of some kind. (No tripe thank goodness! Very bad taste sending me that last year!) I'm starting to mash it all up.

3.47 p.m.   Seems to be a problem at head's end. Everything's grinding to a halt.

3.48 p.m.   Can just hear head arguing.

3.49 p.m.   A whole brussels sprout arrives.

3.55 p.m.   I've started the machinery up again. It's all the same to me, but I wish the sprout had been chewed a bit.

4.30 p.m.   Some of the mixture is ready to move on. Have added loads of acid and other juices. The food has already begun to break down to a soup – it's every colour of the rainbow. Duodenum has relaxed its opening. My walls are starting to squeeze in and squirt the "soup" further on, just as some heavy brown lumps with currants in are being dumped on top of the lot. Cream is steadily dripping down.

5 p.m.   Still hard at work. I'm now stretched like a big J-shaped balloon, contents approximately 1·5 litres. Would you believe anyone could eat so much?

6.30 p.m.   Steady stream of stuff has been arriving from gullet for the last hour and a half. No room to mention everything here. Highlights include crisps, a roast chestnut, a banana, some peanuts, orange juice, savoury biscuits, liquorice, seven

different types of chocolate, and three small sausages (one hardly chewed and you could still see the hole where it was stuck on a stick). I'm beginning to feel a bit tired after the fifth mince pie.

6.45 p.m.   Plate of chips arrives. (Only the chips not the plate!) Even spleen is beginning to feel a bit sorry for me now.

6.55 p.m.   Body went pedalling around the garden in the dark and fell off again. Now it's fighting with our sister.

7.05 p.m.   Head's having a row with our mum over bath time.

7.15 p.m.   We've all been thrown in a hot bath. Some blood had already gone off to help legs with the pedalling. Now more has left me to help skin deal with the hot water. I've had enough. Lungs are breathing fast and my muscles are relaxing ...

7.16 p.m.   Body jumps out of bath ... muscles around me squeeze tight ... mixture is thrown back up through gullet and out of mouth. Ugh! Good riddance.

7.30 p.m.   Body failed to make toilet in time. Most of the mixture was cleaned up quickly, but some acid went on a wool carpet and is starting to burn a hole.

8.30 p.m.   Body feels better. Eyes can see a mince pie and a cucumber sandwich. Mouth is making a bit of saliva. I'm gurgling, but don't feel too bad at all now.

8.40 p.m.   Well chewed mince pie and sandwich have arrived, washed down by some orange juice. I'm starting work again.

9 p.m.   Bed time. I'm empty. The rest of the guts can do some work now. I think I'll turn off the acid and go to sleep – hope I don't have nightmares about Boxing Day.

The stomach is a thick muscular J-shaped bag, with walls which are usually pale when it is empty and pink when digestion is going on. It is the widest part of the whole digestive system – rather like a big cavern in a network of tunnels. Most of it is under your lower ribs on the left side, though its exact position, shape and size vary a lot. It expands as food goes into it. Not surprisingly it is highest in your body when you're empty and lying down, and lowest when you're standing up after eating a big meal. Part of it will then be stretched down well below the level of your belly button.

There is a way in and a way out. Food comes into the stomach from the gullet (oesophagus) and leaves through another tube, the duodenum. When food arrives, the muscles in the stomach walls churn and mix the meal like a washing machine cleaning clothes or a cement mixer making cement. Glands in the walls add strong acid and other digestive juices. Nothing should be able to get out at this stage. At each end, tight circular muscles like elastic bands keep the mixture in until it is ready to be passed on.

The first direct look anyone had at the workings of the stomach was in 1822 when a man called Alexis St Martin was shot in the left side. The hole only partly healed and a Dr William Beaumont found he could use it as a window to see what the stomach got up to.

Beaumont used to dangle various foods on silk threads into St Martin's stomach to see what happened. After a while St Martin got fed up with this and messed up Beaumont's experiments by running away! Life couldn't have been too bad, though, because St Martin got married, had children, and lived to be eighty-two. In fact he outlived Dr Beaumont by fifteen years.

Much more is now known about life inside the stomach. Its muscular walls have a very rich blood supply, and blood is behind much of the way the stomach behaves. Fear makes the walls go pale, because blood is moved away to the muscles, where it can help you escape! When you are angry, on the other hand, your hormones (the chemical messengers in your blood) make your stomach walls (and your face!) go red. If blood is diverted away from the muscles of the stomach wall – perhaps by exercise or a hot bath – then the stomach does not work so well and digestion is slowed down.

One of the busiest days of the year for your stomach is Christmas Day!

A Long and Winding Road

Where in the human body would you most like to live if you had to choose? A friend of mine said the eye. She'd like it there, she said, because you could see everything that was going on. But a strong contender must be the next part of the cucumber sandwich's route – the small intestine, a dark and mysterious tube coiled in the depths of the body.

It's warm and safe in here. Also there's a steady stream of food going by most of the time. A near perfect home – as long as you don't mind the dark. However, moving through it is another matter. Imagine yourself crawling down a dark hot wet tube 250 metres long. This is the equivalent of the journey that the cucumber sandwich has to make in this part of the bowel. And the journey isn't like walking in an open underground tunnel, but much more like having to crawl under a thick warm duvet or blanket, with thick soupy juices seeping down on to you.

The small intestine is like a coiled hosepipe and it runs out of the stomach for some 6 or 7 metres. Laid out straight that's about the same as the length of a school bus or the height of the tallest giraffe – or, put another way, four times the length of the nose of the Statue of Liberty.

The duodenum is the part of the small intestine nearest to the stomach. As the sandwich passes through here, more digestive juices flow in. The food is pushed along by muscles in the intestine walls, like paste being squeezed from a toothpaste tube. You can hear this sometimes as a gurgling squashing sound. The muscles push in regular waves, and this is in fact the way that food is propelled throughout the entire length of the digestive system.

During this stage of the journey most of the valuable parts of the sandwich are absorbed into the body. (By the end of the journey around 95 per cent of goodies will have been taken out of the food.) The small intestine is the area where nearly all the absorption takes place. This is why this section of bowel has to be so long. There's a lot to do to your sandwich during the three hours it takes to pass through here.

The lining of the walls of this part of the bowel is incredibly "fluffy", like a cross between velvet and a towel. The medical term for all the minute finger-like projections is *villi* – this comes from a Latin word meaning "shaggy hair".

If all the villi were laid out flat – and each one of the five million or so is about the size of this comma "," – they would make an area of over 9 square metres. This is five times the area of the skin on the outside of the whole body, if that were laid flat in the same way, and is something like the playing surface of two table tennis tables. And when you consider that these villi have their own microvilli, then the total surface area approaches that of a tennis court – well over 200 square metres. So, as the juices of the small intestine continue to break up the sandwich, there is a huge area for the small broken-down parts of food to ooze across into the body.

Different parts of the food are handled in slightly different ways before they move into the body. The carbohydrates (there are a lot in bread) are broken down into simple sugars such as glucose, and the proteins (there are some in bread and a lot in, for example, meat and cheese) are attacked until they break up into "*amino-acids*" – more about all this later.

The fats (such as the butter or margarine in your sandwich) are broken down into a fine mixture of water and fat. You can see this process – which is called *emulsification* – when washing-up liquid cleans grease off dirty dinner plates. The globules of fat can be seen floating, mixed and dispersed in the washing-up water.

As well as taking in the useful bits of the sandwich, the small intestine also takes back into the body vast amounts of water. In the mixture now is not only the orange juice that you drank with the sandwich, but also a lot of fluid that the body itself made to help with digestion. About 5 litres of fluid are produced in this process every day. It is poured into the mouth as saliva, into the stomach from glands in the stomach wall, and into the duodenum from the liver and a gland called the pancreas. By the time the mixture leaves the small intestine there is only about half a litre of fluid left. A quick bit of maths soon tells you that 4·5 litres have therefore been "mopped up" by the velvety walls of the small intestine.

By the time the food reaches the end of the tunnel little of value is left. What is, moves into the next part of the bowel ready to begin the 1·7-metre journey – at a very much slower pace – to the toilet.

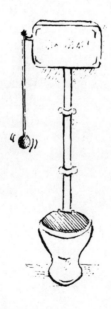

Part Two

Cannibals, Chickens, and Other Problems

Slugs and Snails

What are little boys made of?
What are little boys made of?
Slugs and snails and puppy-dogs' tails,
That's what little boys are made of.

What are little girls made of?
What are little girls made of?
Sugar and spice and all things nice,
That's what little girls are made of.

Apart from as slugs and snails, there are all sorts of other ways of looking at the human body. You can take a photograph to show the outside. There are even very clever ways of picturing the inside with X-rays. But what exactly is it?

One man – Samuel Butler (an English writer born in 1612 who liked to poke fun at the world) – described it as "a pair of pincers set over a bellows and stewpan, with the whole thing mounted on stilts". That's certainly an original way of looking at it!

Other people have had a look at the substances that make up a human body. A detailed chemical analysis of a 65-kilogram grown-up is as follows:

Chemical breakdown of a medium-sized man

WATER	40 kg	61·5%
PROTEIN	11 kg	17 %
FAT	9 kg	14 %
CARBOHYDRATE	1 kg	1·5%
MINERALS	4 kg	6 %

This breakdown is interesting, because, as you would expect, the substances found are the same as those found in food. Water, protein, fat, carbohydrate and minerals all appear in the sandwich. They may not look like a cucumber sandwich any more, and they're not there in the same amounts, but they're there all right, to show that you really are what you eat.

What's happened to the sandwich so far is pretty amazing. What happens next is nothing short of magical.

Cucumbers and Blood

The sandwich has now been digested and absorbed. The next part of the journey is the process of building the sandwich into your body.

As the sandwich moves across the walls of the small intestine, blood is there ready to carry it on a short journey to the liver. Of all the ingredients in the sandwich, the cucumber is the one most at home in the blood. It's literally in its element.

At first any link between a green cucumber and red blood might seem a rather odd one. But really they are more or less made of the same thing – they are both mainly water. In fact the cucumber is 99 per cent water! And this watery cucumber is joining a great deal more water as it becomes part of you, for your body is about two-thirds water. A 65-kilogram man contains about 40 litres of water in all (that's the equivalent of 120 cucumbers!) of which about 5 litres are in the blood (fifteen cucumbers' worth).

The next time you are looking at your teacher, you can picture where those 5 litres are. One litre is travelling out from the heart to the various tissues of the body, and 3 litres are on the way back. And 1 litre (enough to fill two milk bottles) is in the lungs!

The lungs are where the blood picks up oxygen from the air, and where it dumps carbon dioxide, the exhaust fumes of the body. As the oxygen is breathed in, carbon dioxide is breathed out. These two gases don't have much to do with one another when this happens – they just pass by like ships in the night.

Blood is wonderful. It is a vital circulating reservoir of body water. And, as well as carrying cucumber sandwiches and oxygen, it moves all sorts of other vital things around the body. It takes messages contained in chemicals called hormones. Unwanted waste travels to the kidneys in it. It houses many of the body's defences against infection, and it can mobilise this army and quickly transport it to trouble spots. On top of this it's the body's central heating system, carrying "hot water" around you like the pipes to the radiators of a house!

* It is wonderful, too, for writers on the human body because of the amazing facts you can work out about it. A pin prick of it has five million red cells. One red cell takes about ten seconds to travel from your heart to your head and back again. (That's about the time it took you to read from the * at the start of this paragraph to this point!) The return journey to your big toe takes longer – just under a minute. Each red cell lives about 120 days, and in a day travels more than a thousand times around the body.

Finally if all your blood vessels were put end to end they would be long enough to go more than twice around the earth – about 96,560 kilometres (or 386,240,000 cucumbers laid end to end). The sandwich's journey from the intestines to the liver, on the other hand, is a fairly short one – about the length of one cucumber!

Cannibals and the Perfect Diet

Cannibals are people who eat human flesh. (Whether or not they eat cucumber sandwiches too I don't know.) On 20 April 1979 I was sailing off a remote island in the Indian Ocean. Our captain had a book that gave tips about such out-of-the-way places. It was a bit like the travel books that tell car drivers which motorway service stations have toilets, and which serve meals all night, but this book had more exotic information. It warned us that the island had cannibals, and told us to watch out in case they sailed our way in search of lunch. We gave the place a wide berth.

I think the book was a bit out-of-date, looking back on it, but it does show the fear that the term cannibalism brings. It comes from the word Canib, which was the name of a tribe of South Americans who, according to sixteenth-century Spanish explorers, ate human flesh.

In our society cannibalism is very much a "taboo" subject – not something people want to talk about. However, it is part of day-to-day life for many animals. Overcrowding in a trout lake will make some of the larger fish eat the smaller ones. Mice and butterflies will also eat each other under certain conditions. And some female spiders eat their "husbands" to give them extra food to bring up their young spiders!

Humans turn to cannibalism for many reasons. Some people are forced to by starvation. A few tribes have gone on eating humans because their ancestors always have. Occasionally accidents happen. In Tokyo in 1978 a pair of hands from the victim of a gangland killing ended up in the soup pot of a street snack bar. At least fifty innocent customers became cannibals without realising it!

Anyway, the point behind looking at these examples is for us to consider the idea of the human body as food. Various sums have been done with this in mind. One group of experts worked out that an average grown-up would give a meal for 75 cannibals. And gruesome as this thought is, wouldn't a body make the perfect food? Surely if you put a body – after it had been given a good clean-up – through a food processor, then you'd have everything that you could want in a meal. There'd be no need to worry about getting a well balanced diet. All the proteins, minerals, vitamins, and energy foods would be there on your plate in exactly the right amounts.

There are a number of reasons why this wouldn't

work. One obvious one is the problem of getting enough bodies. (Some South American tribes do eat their dead, and it is considered a very respectful way to deal with the deceased – much better, they think, than burying them in the ground or burning them.)

Perhaps the main problem is that eating human flesh regularly seems to be bad for you. Not everything is understood about this yet, but the disease of kuru is a particularly nasty problem linked with cannibalism.

Kuru is a disease of the brain. It leads first to shaky movements which get worse and worse, and eventually, three to six months later, to madness and death.

Don't worry about getting this. It has only been found among tribal people in a remote highland area of central New Guinea.

Doctors had a close look at this mysterious illness when it was first discovered, and experiments seemed to show that the condition was somehow spread if brain tissue was passed on from one being to another. How this could happen wasn't exactly clear at first. However, as cannibalism was stamped out in New Guinea, kuru disappeared as well. It now seems certain that whatever causes kuru is passed on by eating human brains.

Kuru is just one of many good reasons for not becoming a cannibal, and luckily it isn't necessary to eat other humans – you can turn any meal into you. Your body does this with the aid of your very own perfect food processor – your liver.

As the cucumber sandwich arrives at the liver, it is pulling into the biggest internal organ of the body. A grown-up's liver – as long as it hasn't been damaged by drinking too much alcohol – weighs about 1·5 kilograms. This means it's four times the weight of the heart. It's a magnificent piece of equipment. Not only does it take in the sandwich, but it can store some of it, change bits if necessary, and send other parts off around the body. And if there were any poisons in the sandwich it would sort these out too. Another way of describing the liver is as a chemical factory. It really is the ultimate in food processors.

The sandwich has already been broken down by digestion. Now your liver begins to sort the ingredients. These include *fats*, *sugars*, *protein*, *minerals* and *vitamins*.

8

Chips with Everything

Dear Doctor pete

School The woman at
~~School~~ who does the meals
Says if I eat any more chips
I'll ~~start~~ to look like one. we
all love chips. Could you live
on them if you wanted to?
She also says our class eats
too many sweets.

yours sincerely

Sarah

There has been one case of a person who lived only on potatoes. In 1913 a Danish keep-fit enthusiast survived for three hundred days, and all he ate each day was 4 kilograms of potatoes and a little margarine.

He managed to do this because potatoes are an extremely good food. As well as containing energy-giving carbohydrate in the form of starch, they have some protein, just enough vitamins, and fibre.

However, it is not a very good – or practical – idea to try this yourself. When you are growing you need much more than the potato – or any other one food – can supply. If you ate only potato, you might start to look pale like a potato, but you won't ever look like a chip!

As a matter of interest there's hardly any fat in potatoes (if you don't fry them, of course). People are often surprised by this because they think just plain potatoes make you "fat". It's actually very unfair to label the potato fattening. If you eat too many and don't use up the energy in them, then the body will turn this energy into fat. But this is true of all foods, not just the potato.

You don't say what sort of sweets the school dinner lady tells you off about. Sweets taste "sweet" because they have sugars in them. Like the starch in the potato, sugar is an important part of the body's energy supply. If you eat sugars in moderation and burn off the energy then they won't make you fat.

However, there is one great danger with sugars – they may cause holes in teeth. There is a link between the number of sweets a person eats and how many fillings the dentist has to put into that person's mouth. The reason is that bacteria living in the mouth feed off the sugar and then produce an acid which "eats" into the teeth. Cleaning teeth helps stop this. At one time in the United Kingdom eight out of every ten children starting school had holes in their teeth. Dentists have quite a job pulling 4 tonnes of teeth out of children's mouths every year – though somehow it's hard to feel sorry for them!

The nagging from your dinner lady is all really about your intake of carbohydrates. These you get from many different foods – not just potatoes and sweets – and they give the body fuel to run on. They supply much of our energy. They are like the petrol in a car, or the coal in a steam train.

Carbohydrates

There are three kinds of carbohydrates, all of which are contained in plants. These are sugars, starches, and cellulose.

Cellulose is the fibre which gives plants such as our cucumber their shape. Without cellulose they would be like a human with no bones, or a chocolate figure melting on a hot day. Cellulose can't be absorbed by our intestines, but it is very important because it provides roughage for the bowel to work on and push against.

Sugars are produced in plants from the sun's energy and can be used by the plants as an immediate source of energy, for example for growing new leaves. Sucrose is the type of sugar extracted from sugar cane and sugar beet. Closely related are fructose from fruit, lactose from milk, and other sugars such as glucose and maltose.

Starch is the energy store of plants. The potato, for example, uses sugars to make starch and then stores this in itself. If the potato stays in the ground the energy is there ready to grow new potatoes the next year. But if you dig it up and eat it, you get the energy.

9

Cows Are Vegetarians

Dear Doctor pete

A lady at School says you will get a big bottom from sitting around a lot. I go horse-riding and my brother Edward is always on his bike. Are we going to end up with big behinds?

Yours sincerely

Sarah

P.S. It's the same person I wrote to you about last week — the one who goes on about chips and sweets.

You will not get a big bottom from sitting around too much. A lot of grown-ups have jobs where they sit around all day at desks. Gluteus maximus is the muscle they sit on. It's already the biggest one in the human body. Imagine all the enormous bottoms coming home from the office if what your dinner lady said were true.

The bottom is mainly muscle, made of protein, and it is true that muscles do increase in size with use.

Champion tennis players often have bigger muscles in the arm that they use to hold their racket. But just sitting on a muscle won't make it bigger. It may get squashed, but when you stand up it'll go back into shape.

Muscles have to be exercised really hard to make them enlarge. The mind boggles about what bits of the body would expand if over-use alone made them bigger. The tongue is made of muscle – but most teachers and dinner ladies have the same sized tongues as the rest of us.

Here's a trick to show your dinner lady:

How to Turn a Sandwich into Your Arm

1 Make a cucumber sandwich. Put some cheese in it to increase the amount of protein (there's already a bit in the bread).
2 Eat it.
3 Wait a few days.
4 Hey presto. The protein from the sandwich is now part of the protein in the muscles of your arm (by weight the arm is mainly muscle, though it has nerves, blood, fat and bone, as well as skin to cover it all).

Protein

You need a regular supply of protein. It makes up 10 per cent of your body weight and is contained in every cell of the body. Your cells have to be continually replaced and repaired – it's been worked out that all of them, apart from those in brain and teeth, are replaced on average every seven years. And until about the age of eighteen you are still growing – during these years you need even more protein so that you can build new cells as well as repairing old ones.

Protein is made up of a number of amino-acids *strung together like beads. When your sandwich was being digested in the small intestine this "string" was dissolved, and now the individual "beads" have reached your liver they are joined together again in new strings to build the protein of your own body.*

The twenty or so different amino-acids that form your body proteins are rather like the letters of the alphabet. The proteins made from them are like words. The "words" fit together in such a way that each individual person is unique, just as the words in this book are arranged to make each sentence different from the others.

Some of the amino-acids that make up human protein have to be manufactured in the body by converting the amino-acids that are obtained from food. Other essential ones can't be made but must be eaten in exactly the right form. Meat, cheese, milk, eggs, fish, beans, and nuts are all good sources of protein. And it is worth saying that a vegetarian – someone who does not eat meat – of course gets a perfectly good supply of protein. Cows develop very good muscle. And they are vegetarians.

10

Fat as a Pig

Dear Doctor Pete

Sorry to bother you again. My brother eats all the time. He's as fat as a pig. Would cucumber sandwiches make him lose weight?

yours sincerely

Sarah

P.S. The school dinner lady has had a heart attack. She's in hospital.

In 1866 two scientists called Lawes and Gilbert took a close look at dead pigs. They measured the fat in these pigs and found more of it than the animals had eaten in their entire lives. It was obvious from this that at least some fat must have been made from another substance. This gave a clue to one way human beings collect fat in their bodies.

Fat is used by the body to give energy. If you eat more than you need immediately, the body stores it for leaner times. Carbohydrates (sugars and starch) are also used to give instant energy, but these too are turned into fat stores if more are eaten than are needed at the time. This is because fat is the best, most space-saving way to store energy. A piece of fat produces twice the energy of the same weight of carbohydrate. So some of the fat in the pigs' bodies had been formed from carbohydrates.

It was vital for our ancestors to be able to store food and energy like this. They had to hunt for food, and used a lot more energy than we do now. And there could be times when food was scarce. Their reserves of fat then kept them going until the next meal came along.

So fats are crucial, and there's more to them than simply that they make your brother wobble. They are especially important as energy for young people who are growing and charging around everywhere.

However, many people eat more food than they need and do not burn it up with exercise. This is especially true of grown-ups who have stopped growing. A lumberjack uses a lot of energy chopping down trees, but many of us have jobs that involve little more exercise than driving to and from work and sitting behind a desk. So, as most of us do not lead the active lives of our ancestors, the danger is that fat can build up in obvious places and can make us "fat". (I don't mean to be unkind, but when was the last time your dinner lady ran around the playground for half an hour or chopped down a tree?)

As well as making the body heavier, fats can put the body under strain in another way. Too much of some fats, if eaten over many years, can cause heart attacks. The fats "fur up" the blood vessels. These become damaged and narrow and the heart can't pump the blood·through them. (Other things make heart attacks more likely, as well. Smoking cigarettes is one of the worst, and stress and worry are bad too.)

Quite what is happening to your brother's body depends on what he's eating, and how much exercise he's taking to burn any extra food away. He's not going to have a heart attack now, but he could be storing up trouble for later life.

A cucumber sandwich, without anything else in it, doesn't contain much energy – compared with something like a slice of meat pie and chips. If your brother did cut out some calories (energy in food is measured in calories) by changing what he ate, then he might lose some weight. This doesn't mean he should change over to living on cucumber sandwiches alone. This sort of weird diet is just as bad as eating the wrong foods. A well balanced diet is the thing to aim for.

It also does not mean that cutting out food is the only way to stay healthy and trim. If you take regular exercise you use up excess food as energy. It then does not turn into body stores of fat.

Here's an interesting idea about food and calories and losing weight. Different foods – whatever they are – contain different numbers of calories. Celery has very few calories in it – even fewer than cucumbers. In fact the process of eating celery actually uses up more energy than there is in the celery. So even if you continually ate celery, all day and all night, you would slowly lose weight. This is not a good idea – even if you are keen on celery! It's just a good way to understand the energy cycle, and how you need a certain number of calories each day to live.

Fat

Fat is one of the most misunderstood parts of food. One reason is that people mean different things by "fat". To some people it means butter, lard and the white covering on meat. To others fat is what hangs over your belt as a "spare tyre" if you eat too much. Scientists – as you might expect – have a much more complicated understanding of "fat".

Fats are made up of molecules (tiny particles) of oxygen, carbon, and hydrogen – the same oxygen that you breathe, the same carbon that makes up coal and the same hydrogen that was used to make airships float. There's nothing else to them. It is the numbers of these molecules and the way they are linked up that makes them into fats. (These three molecules also make up the carbohydrates – sugar and starch – but here they are arranged in a different order.)

Fat in food is needed by the body for a number of reasons, not just to provide energy. Some fats contain vitamins not found anywhere else. Fats are essential for building the walls of every cell in the body. Fats are needed to make hormones (the important chemical messengers which travel around in the blood). Fat also protects the body from cold – it's a very good "blanket" and it makes a good packing material to protect your insides.

Most of us can picture the obvious fats – foods such as margarine and meat fat. However, there are a lot of fats which are not so obvious. Peanuts, for example, are half fat. Foods which have no fats include most vegetables, sugar, egg white, and most drinks which do not have milk in them.

Find the Fat

You can usually find fat in food with a simple experiment:

1 Cut up some brown wrapping paper into squares.
2 Select the foods you wish to test. To start with, try a slice of raw cucumber, a slice of cheese, and a slice of raw potato.
3 Label each square of paper with the name of a food, and then rub that food on to it.
4 Let the paper dry, and then hold it up to the light. Light will shine through the paper if the food contained fat.

Of these three foods, you will find it is only the cheese which contains fat. You can see this effect in real life in the paper used to sell fish and chips. This food has a lot of fat, and you can almost see through the paper where the fat has soaked in.

However, and this is important, white fish and potato chips uncooked have hardly any fat in them. The fat has come in the cooking. They were fried in fat. So when working out how much fat you are eating you have to think about how your food is prepared.

It is not correct to label fat – or any single food with fat in it – as "bad". What is "bad" or for that matter "good" is how much fat and what kind of fat is part of a person's regular diet.

The whole business of fats in food can be quite baffling, especially the difference between *saturated* and *unsaturated* fats. But there is a fairly straightforward guideline. Fats which are hard at room temperature, including butter and the fat on beef, lamb and pork, are usually saturated. Fats which are liquid or very soft at room temperature – such as sunflower margarine, corn and sunflower cooking oil – are generally unsaturated. One difference between these two types of fat is in the way the oxygen, carbon and hydrogen are linked together. What's more important than this, however, is the difference between what these two sorts of fats can do to your body. Excess saturated fats tend to make the arteries clog up. This is an important cause of heart attacks. (Although a lot of meat is high in saturated fats, fish and poultry are not, so it isn't true to label all animal foods as being bad for you.)

The lesson of fats and being fat is that you must be careful of what you eat. Enjoy all foods in moderation, and burn off the energy with exercise.

11

A Letter from Edward

Dear Dr Pete I hear from my sister that you are writing a book about cucumbers. I've never had a cucumber and I don't Like them! what about other sandwiches?

Love

Edward

You can have what you like in your sandwich. Although this is the adventure of a cucumber sandwich it could be about any food that you have eaten. But it's worth being careful not to miss out on food that you really might like if you tried it. Many people are scared of certain foods for no good cause. (Is it really worth starting a fight over a brussels sprout?) The story of the tomato and the potato is a good example of how some excellent foods can get a bad name.

The History of the Tomato and the Potato – A Couple of Dangerous Cousins?

The first tomato plants arrived in Europe from South America in the sixteenth century. They were brought back by explorers and must have been a yellow variety since they were called "golden apples" at the time.

At first the soft pulpy colourful fruits were very popular. But then people began to believe that they were bad for you. It's not that uncommon for a food to become unpopular without a particular reason. The downfall – for a while – of the tomato may have been because it's related to the deadly nightshade and other poisonous plants. In fact the leaves and stems of tomato plants do contain a poison called solanine.

Eventually it was shown once and for all that the tomatoes themselves were not deadly poisonous, and were great to eat. After this they were not only regarded as food, but also as medicine. Tomato ketchup was sold as a medicine in America in the 1830s – Dr Miles's Compound Extract of Tomato!

The potato, a cousin of the tomato, was another plant that originally came from America. It was brought to England by Sir Walter Raleigh in 1586. When potatoes were first eaten by friends of Sir Walter Raleigh and Queen Elizabeth, the cooks used the leaves and stems. These gave the court belly ache and it took another hundred or so years before the value of potatoes began to be realised.

Now what was once considered poisonous is one of the most popular foods in the world – whether baked, boiled, roasted for Sunday lunch, or made into packets of crisps.

12

The Strange Case of the Loony Chickens

Chickens are funny birds. They're blind at night because their eyes can't work in the dark, and they've been known to run around alive with their heads chopped off!

This makes it all the more remarkable that a doctor called Eijkman should recognise some odd behaviour of theirs as a vital clue to a mysterious disease in humans.

In 1897 Christian Eijkman was working in Indonesia. He was a Dutch doctor at a military hospital. A number of his sick patients had a condition called beriberi. Beriberi had become common in the Far East during the mid nineteenth century – about the time that steam-driven mills were introduced there to remove the tough brown husks from rice. Since then, polished white rice had come to replace brown rice in the daily diet of many people.

At the time there was no reason to link the new mills to beriberi. In fact no one knew quite what beriberi was, except that you were very ill and weak with it, and had strange feelings like pins and needles being stuck in your skin. However, Eijkman noticed that the people who got beriberi ate this polished rice, and he tried feeding some chickens with white rice from the officers' mess. They soon began to behave very strangely. Their legs went weak, and they started walking about the place with their heads drawn in.

While Eijkman was puzzling over this, a new head cook arrived and stopped him feeding the chickens polished rice. It was considered too good for them. So Eijkman began to feed them their usual unmilled rice again. To his amazement they made a sudden and miraculous recovery from their mystery condition. They were soon up and about, and strutting around with their heads stuck out as normal. Eijkman realised that the chickens had begun to suffer from something very like beriberi when they were fed on polished rice, and somehow the unpolished rice had put this right.

Beriberi was beginning to be understood at last, although it wasn't until 1936 that vitamin B1 (thiamine) was found to be the key missing ingredient. This is contained in the inner husk of rice, and the steam mills were removing it as they processed the rice. Dr Eijkman received the Nobel Prize for what he found out about chickens and vitamin B1.

Vitamin C, needed to make blood vessels, bones and teeth, and to keep these parts of the body in good working order, is another vitamin with an interesting history. It's the reason the British are often called "Limeys" by the Americans.

In 1753 a Dr James Lind did an experiment on twelve sailors with the disease of scurvy. Scurvy had been a dreadful problem for seafarers for thousands of years. In fact in the 1700s it killed more sailors than drowning, pirates and sea battles put together. If you got it you became very unwell – your teeth fell out, your gums bled, and bruises appeared for no apparent reason. In fact most parts of the body were damaged in one way or another. If children got it their bones stopped growing. And no one knew what caused it.

Lind's twelve sailors were at sea on board the same ship. He put them in pairs and gave each pair a different "treatment". Some of these treatments were pretty awful. One pair got sea water, another vinegar, and another sulphuric acid. The luckier ones got cider, or a mixture of garlic and mustard. The really lucky pair got two oranges and a lemon.

The two on the oranges and lemon were back at work in a week. The pair on the cider (from apples) felt a bit better. But the others stayed ill with scurvy.

This was the beginning of understanding that scurvy was caused by a lack of something which was in fruit. At that time sailors went without fruit because there was no way of keeping it fresh on long voyages.

It still took a while to get things perfectly right even after this experiment had shown the good that fruit could do. The English navy provided lime juice for its sailors (hence "Limey") because lemon juice was more expensive. Lime juice could be bought cheaply in the West Indies. Sadly lime juice has only a third of the vitamin C of lemon juice and so many sailors still suffered from scurvy.

As other vitamins were discovered at various times,

they were each named after a letter of the alphabet. A lot is now known about them. Vitamin B was once thought to be just one substance. Now it's known to be a group of at least twelve. B1 is the one the loony chickens in Indonesia needed. Other B vitamins are needed to keep blood healthy and for turning food (such as your cucumber sandwich) into energy that your body can use. They're found in all sorts of foods ranging from meats to cereals and vegetables.

Vitamin A is needed to keep skin and eyes healthy and to make strong bones. It's found in cheese, oily fish, milk, eggs, butter and margarine, and it can be made in your body from a yellowy substance called carotene which is found in carrots, tomatoes and many other vegetables.

Vitamin K helps blood clot. Without it you may bleed a great deal after a small cut. It's found in a whole host of foods, such as cereals, nuts, fruit and liver, as well as green vegetables.

Vitamin D is needed to form healthy bones and teeth. Young people who go without it may get rickets. They'll have bow legs because their soft bones can't support their body weight and so become bent and twisted. (The name rickets comes from "wrikken", an English word from the Middle Ages, which means "to twist".)

There was quite a bit of detective work involved in the discovery of vitamin D, too. In 1919 it was found that sunlight and cod liver oil could each cure rickets. It has been discovered that cod liver oil works because it has a lot of the vitamin in it. Sitting in the sun works because the body itself can produce the vitamin in the skin, but it needs to be in the sunlight to do so.

In the last century about 75 per cent of children living in some city slums had rickets. The reason was partly their poor diet, and partly because high buildings all around them and smoke from factories cut out much of the sunlight. (Normally about 90 per cent of vitamin D is made by the body, and the other 10 per cent comes from food.) Things got better when laws cut down on the smoke and when many children started to be given cod liver oil. By 1945 rickets was rare in Britain, but doctors still have to keep an eye out for it.

The different vitamins are all extremely important. They may only be needed in very small amounts, but your body has to have them if it is to work properly. "Vitamin" comes from the word "vita", which means "life", and vitamins really are essential for healthy life.

How to Make an "Iron Nail" out of a Sandwich

Method:

1 Make a sandwich.
2 Eat the sandwich, and drink some orange juice.
3 Wait a few days.
4 Iron from the food will now be part of your body. In total there's enough in the average body to make an iron nail about 7 centimetres long!

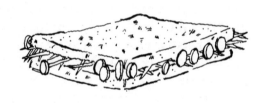

What you will need:

1 Food with iron in.
   The 4 grams of iron in the body come from all sorts of foods. Black treacle and curry powder happen to have quite a bit! It doesn't matter if you are not eating huge quantities of these, though, because lots of other foods contain iron.

There's iron in meat (especially liver and black pudding), nuts, beans, peas and bread, so nut pâté or liver sausage would go well with the cucumber in this sandwich. It's sometimes surprising where the iron is. A kilogram of digestive biscuits has the same amount of iron as a kilogram of roast beef. Fruit gums and liquorice also contain a lot.

No single food is likely to supply you with all the iron you need. (If you are between ten and twelve years old you need about 12 milligrams of iron a day.) You'll get all you require from a well balanced mixture of foods.

2   Your digestive system.

Iron is taken into the body across the walls of the small intestine after the food leaves the stomach. Once inside it's distributed to various places. About one-third of your body iron is stored in the liver.

Most of the rest is in the red blood cells. (Two teaspoons of blood have about 5 milligrams of iron.) It is "haemoglobin" that actually makes the blood red, and this is made up of an iron compound (haem) and a protein called globin. Its job is to carry oxygen around the body.

A small, but very important, amount of iron is also needed in the chemical reaction that builds up molecules of stored energy.

Not all iron in food can be easily absorbed into the body. Vitamin C is one of the most important additions to a meal when you need to take in plenty of iron (hence the glass of orange juice with your sandwich).

Iron is just one of the minerals in the body. Another is the metal zinc. Like the iron, you'll get all the zinc you need to run your body properly as long as you eat a mixed diet. There are about 2 grams of it in a grown-up. (As a matter of interest zinc pops up in some other unexpected places. As well as being in torch batteries, and TV screens, it's also the soothing ingredient of calamine lotion. There's enough zinc in an adult to make about 50 millilitres of the lotion. That's about enough to cover an itchy face.)

Other minerals in the body in tiny amounts are iodine, fluorine, copper, cobalt, chromium, manganese, selenium, molybdenum, vanadium, nickel, silicon, lithium, boron, tin, aluminium, lead, mercury, and cadmium. Your body also holds a real surprise – arsenic. However, it's only in a minute quantity and is not in a form that will harm you. Shellfish is the food with most arsenic!

The body is very good at taking what it needs from food, and getting rid – usually in urine – of what it doesn't want. But it is important to stop the world becoming even more polluted. For if it does, some substances which are safe in small amounts could get into the body in poisonous quantities. And the story behind the Mad Hatter shows how nasty this can be. Years ago, people who dyed the felt for hats would get "hatter's shakes" and then would slowly go quite mad. "Mad as a hatter" became a common expression, and this is what gave Lewis Carroll the idea for his famous character in *Alice in Wonderland*. But the reason for the shakes and the madness was in fact poisoning – mercury from the dye was absorbed slowly over many years until this metal, which is harmless in tiny quantities, collected in the body in dangerous amounts.

Sadly mercury poisoning still occurs in the world. Only a few years ago there was an outbreak in Japan. Industry polluted the water of Minamata Bay and this affected the fish. When these were caught and eaten people started suffering from mercury poisoning. At first it was a mystery, but eventually the source of the pollution was traced back along the chain to the factories.

Part Three

You Are What You Eat

14

Worth Your Weight in Gold?

Eating a cucumber sandwich is a fairly easy thing to do. And once you've done it you can leave your body to get on and turn the food into you without your brain having to think about it consciously any more.

But what if a scientist had to make a human body from the raw materials contained in the sandwich? It's been worked out that just to make the building blocks for a body – the proteins and fats – would cost several hundreds of millions of pounds, even if it could be done. And that's before they are assembled into cells. There is an astronomical price quoted for putting these together and making a single body cell, and there are about seventy-five million million (that is, seventy-five trillion) cells in the human body!

However, in case you're feeling rather valuable all of a sudden, you can work out what could be made from YOU. (And as a bit of fun you could add up what each item would cost to buy.)

Already it's clear that there's an iron nail to be had out of the human body, and a small bottle of calamine lotion. There's quite a lot else, too, that in theory you could make.

There is enough hydrogen in your teacher to fill a balloon which could lift him or her to the top of the Eiffel Tower. Your teacher won't float off – you will be relieved to hear – because the body hydrogen is in use in another form. Two molecules of it are linked to every oxygen molecule to make the body's water

(H_2O). A fully grown teacher will have 40 kilograms of water in him or her. This is 40 litres – about enough to have a bath in.

There's enough fat in an average person to make seven large bars of soap. There's enough sugar to fill a jam jar. If you wanted some salt then there's enough in a human body to fill six salt cellars. There's enough carbon – around 13 kilograms – to make nine thousand pencil leads.

Sulphur is present in the body. Most is bound up in two of the amino-acids that make up the body's protein. There is enough in these amino-acids (170 grams) to kill all the fleas on a dog.

The phosphorus – mainly in bones as phosphate – could make 2,200 match heads. The body's potassium – mainly inside cell water – could explode a toy cannon.

If you did have to go out and buy all these various items they wouldn't actually cost very much. You'd just have, among other things, enough soap for a year and enough pencils to last a lifetime. So if you are ever feeling rather precious or too important it's worth remembering that in one way you're not worth much more than this book.

No one, as far as I know, has ever seriously thought of making different cells, and then building them into a brain, a heart, a liver, two lungs and two kidneys, 5 litres of blood, 9 metres of bowels, 206 bones, over 600 muscles, and, to finish off, a covering of skin. Just thinking about how difficult it would be makes the process of digestion and what follows seem even more remarkable.

So far in this amazing journey the sandwich has been prepared by the body ready for use. This next part is about what the various organs, such as the brain, the lungs and the heart, do with the sandwich once it's inside you. For they are made out of all the food you consume. You are what you eat!

15

Mussels with Muscles

What is the link between the following – a giant clam trapping a diver's leg until he drowns, being able to hold a crocodile's mouth shut, and the fact that your heart will beat about 3,363,840,000 times during your life?* The answer is that they're all amazing facts you probably didn't know about muscles. (That's muscles as in Tarzan, not as in shellfish!)

*80 (beats per minute) × 60 (minutes) × 24 (hours) × 365 (days) × 80 (years) = 3,363,840,000

Muscles are responsible for everything from closing that clam's mouth, to operating the jaws of the crocodile, and to making your heart beat. They make up a large part of you – about 40 per cent of the weight of a man and 35 per cent of a woman is muscle. You have well over six hundred muscles in your body – walking uses more than two hundred.

All animals have some sort of muscle arrangement. Even worms. Worms have two sets of muscles – one makes the worm long and thin, and the other makes it short and fat. When these two work against each other the worm moves along.

In man, most of the muscles that move the body are attached to bone. They tend to work in pairs. One muscle pulls against the other. It is an important working arrangement with muscles that they always pull. In fact they can't push. Even when you are pushing something, a combination of muscles is in fact pulling.

Although the teams of muscles work in pairs, one movement may not be as strong as its opposite. You can close your jaws with incredible force, although opening your mouth is not nearly such a powerful action. Try it. The crocodile is similar, which is useful to know in case you get cornered by one. The crocodile can close its jaws with tremendous force – if you tried to prise them open it would be like trying to move a couple of snoozing African elephants. But the muscles that open the jaws are quite weak. A human can easily hold them shut. So the trick is to catch your crocodile with its mouth closed and keep it like that.

The muscles that work the crocodile's jaws are known as "voluntary" muscles – that is, the crocodile has them under direct control. It can bite when it chooses – just as we can pick up and eat our sandwich when we like. Other muscles, you may not be surprised to know, are called "involuntary" because they work without you having to tell them to. The heart muscle is in this group, so you don't have to think about making it beat each one of those 3,363,840,000 times. (Imagine what would happen during sleep otherwise.) The muscles that squeezed the cucumber sandwich along the intestines are like this, too – they don't need a direct instruction from you in order to work.

The heart really is the most amazing muscle. It may not be the strongest in the body, but it must take some kind of record for working without fail throughout your entire life. This hollow double-barrelled pump about the size of your fist, beats sixty to eighty times a minute, and shifts about 5 litres of blood around the body during that time. It keeps up this incredible work rate, without a rest, day and night, for over seventy years. The work done by the heart in five hundred days is what it would take to lift one of those African elephants to the top of Mount Everest.

When muscles work they get hot. In fact, one of their jobs is to make heat to keep the body warm. Just sitting chatting produces an amazing amount – twelve people talking in a room give off the same heat as a one-bar electric fire. In a day an adult makes enough heat to melt about 30 litres of ice and then to boil that water!

Whatever sort of muscle it is – an involuntary one in the intestines or a voluntary one in the arm or leg – the energy needed for it to work comes from food. Not all animals eat cucumber sandwiches – worms, giant clams, and crocodiles don't usually – but they all have some kind of similar energy supply. Foods differ in how much energy they have in them. A large sandwich with a mixture of fillings may have around 300 Calories. There are about the same number in a bar of chocolate.

This is what you can do on 300 Calories:

Sleep for just over	4 hours
Sit in a chair reading this book or peel potatoes for	3 hours
Wash dishes or walk the dog for	1 hour
Make your bed for	45 minutes
Ride a bike or dance for	40 minutes
Swim for	30 minutes
Ski on hard level snow	25 minutes

These figures are not exact. They can't be, as every person is different. (Men, for example, use a lot more energy washing up and peeling potatoes than women!) Also you swim and dance in different ways from your friends. However, the average ten-year-old needs about 2,500 Calories a day. A 300-Calorie sandwich or a bar of chocolate only gives about one-eighth (12 per cent) of this.

There are plenty of amazing facts about muscles. You use 17 to smile and 43 to frown. (So save energy and smile.) They are strongest when we are around twenty-five. The biggest in the human body is the gluteus maximus (bottom or buttock to you and me) and the smallest – 0·12 centimetres long – is attached to the smallest bone of the body, inside the ear. This is all very useful information if you are stuck for something to say at a party!

As for the giant clam and its muscles, I was brought up to believe that these eat men – or at least trap unwary divers by the legs. Giant clams are quite common in the Indian Ocean and Pacific, and the shells can weigh as much as 250 kilograms and be well over a metre long. Pearls the size of tennis balls have been discovered in them.

If you examine one it is easy to see how the stories arose. The wavy edges of the shells fit together tightly when closed, and the mussel's muscles that do this are immensely strong. However, these giant molluscs are easy to see, and they can only close their shells slowly because of the great quantity of water that has to be moved in the process. So, despite being mentioned as a danger in countless adventure stories, and even in the United States Navy Diving Manual, the truth is that there is no recorded case anywhere of a diver being trapped and drowned by a giant clam.

Skiing on Cucumbers

People often make jokes about cucumbers. I've really no idea why. Just because you're long and green doesn't mean you should be laughed at. And being green is rather fashionable these days!

However, at the risk of adding to these jokes, I have to ask a serious question. How can you ski on a cucumber sandwich? Surely a sandwich is rather a floppy thing? Cucumbers themselves are harder – but not hard enough to ski on. Yet this food has become part of a human body which is solid enough to ski down mountains.

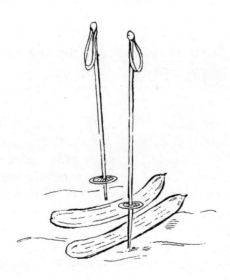

The answer must lie somehow in the bones. There are over two hundred of them in your body, of all shapes and sizes – flat, long, pebble-shaped, cup-shaped – and they have a number of jobs. Some bones protect internal organs – the flat bones on the top of your head enclose the brain, and the ribs make a cage around your heart and lungs. Others have very special jobs – the 3-millimetre-long stirrup-shaped stapes (the shortest bone in the body), is one of three bones within each ear which help carry sound to the brain.

Most bones, however, are part of a framework on which the organs of the body are hung for support. Crabs and lobsters have their bones on the outside. We have ours on the inside. They are like internal scaffolding. Without bones the body would be as shapeless as a jellyfish stranded on a beach.

The femur is the longest bone in the body. It runs from the hip to the knee, making up over a quarter of the height of an adult (a 183-centimetre, or 6-foot, man will have femurs about 50 centimetres long). The way it's constructed is fairly typical of a long bone and goes some way to explain how the body is strong enough to ski.

There is a joint at either end, at the hip and the knee, and between the two is a tube of bone. Because it isn't solid bone right to the middle, it is light and easy to move. The centre of some long bones – including those that make up the arms and legs – is full of bone marrow, a softer substance in which most of the body's red blood cells are made.

The strength of the femur lies partly in the basic tube design. You can see how this works using a piece of writing paper. Roll it into a tube and put an elastic band around to keep it this shape. You'll be able to balance quite a heavy book on top without it crumpling.

However, bones don't just have to be strong, they have to be flexible, too – otherwise there would be a danger of them snapping like dry twigs. Just as the Eiffel Tower needs to bend slightly in high winds, so bones need to "give" when under the stress of everyday activities such as standing and walking – and when it comes to skiing, the femurs have to bend like longbows.

Bone tissue manages to do this because one of its main ingredients is a gristly protein which is quite flexible. Your outer ear – the part that you can see on the side of your head – is made of this gristle. But there is more to bones than simply gristle, which brings us back to the question of how a soft sandwich can turn into such a strong, tough part of the body. The key to the puzzle is the calcium in food. Crystals of calcium are sown like seeds in the bendy protein, and calcium gives bone its hardness.

Ninety-nine per cent of the body calcium is contained in the bones of the skeleton. (There is an important 1 per cent, though, which is needed for other jobs, apart from making bones and teeth. It controls the correct working of the nervous system, and is involved in clotting blood.)

When you are about twelve you need just under 1 gram of calcium a day. This is about the amount in three glasses of milk, or in a lump of hard cheese the size of a snooker ball. (If you are a few years younger you won't need quite so much.) You can get calcium from a balanced mixture of different foods. Cheese and milk are rich in it, but many other foods, such as eggs, bread and nuts, have some too.

After you have eaten your sandwich some of the calcium – not all – is taken into the blood across the wall of the small intestine. It joins a reserve "pool" of calcium already in the blood. If you weighed this in an adult it would be just under 1 gram – compared to around 1,200 grams of calcium in the skeleton.

The blood and the bones are in continual contact, and calcium moves to and fro like people moving freely across the border between a small country and a much bigger neighbour. The bones are continually being remodelled and kept in top shape by this process – in fact about 20 grams of your skeleton is "knocked down" and then rebuilt each day. So, far from being like some dry old dusty bones in a churchyard or a museum, your skeleton is changing all the time like a living coral reef.

17

A Lot of Hot Air

On 18 August 1974 the world's largest hot air balloon took off. It had 14,000 cubic metres of air in it – less than half the air you will breathe into your lungs in a lifetime.

This total can be worked out as follows. Every breath AT REST takes in about 0·4 litres of air, and AT REST you breathe about twelve times a minute. So:

in one minute	you breathe about	5 l
in one hour	you breathe about	300 l
in one day	you breathe about	7,200 l
in one year	you breathe about	2,628,000 l
in 70 years	you breathe about	183,960,000 l

This is 183,960 cubic metres of air – over 13 times the volume of that balloon. In twenty-four hours at rest you take in enough air to fill around three telephone boxes, and on a normal day (you are not always resting!) you breathe in enough to fill six.

This is a lot of air. And as one-fifth of air is oxygen, it is also a lot of oxygen – it's just as well that oxygen is the most plentiful element in our world, making up nearly half the earth's crust, for we must have oxygen to live.

When you breathe in, the rib cage and a flat muscle underneath it called the "diaphragm" work rather like a pair of bellows to draw air into the two lungs. The lungs, inside the rib cage, are like large pinky-white sponges. In an adult, each one is about the size of a rugby ball. This may not seem very big for what they do, but there are about 300 million tiny air sacs – alveoli – within the lungs.

These minute alveoli are grouped together like small bunches of grapes, and contain a network of tiny blood vessels. This is where oxygen from the air gets into the blood. If all the alveoli were flattened out they would cover about 143 square metres. This is about a hundred times the area of your skin if that were flattened out, and more than the area of half a tennis court. This huge area, packed inside your chest, gives the blood plenty of space to pick up oxygen. If the area is reduced, for example by smoking damaging the lungs, the body has to breathe faster to get enough oxygen. Unfortunately once the lungs have been damaged like this there is no way of putting them right.

When the oxygen has been taken into the blood, the heart pumps it all around the body. The blood vessels that carry the blood and its oxygen are like the road network of a country. Roads may not run right to everyone's front door, but the milkman can get to

every house or flat along some path or other. In the body's case, every cell that needs it gets oxygen by some route.

All this happens very smoothly, day and night. You don't have to think about it. A control centre deep in the brain operates the breathing muscles – unless you consciously choose to interfere. So when you run a race in the school sports, your breathing automatically speeds up to keep pace with the increased need for oxygen. In fact when you exercise, your muscles will need around fifty times more oxygen every minute than when you are at rest. Here is how this is possible:

1 Blood flow through the lungs and from the heart increases by *six* times, from 5 litres per minute to 30 litres per minute.
2 *Three* times as much blood is sent to the muscles – it is diverted from areas such as the skin and intestines to where it is now needed most.
3 *Three* times as much oxygen is taken from the blood by the muscles.

$$6 \times 3 \times 3 = 54$$

So fifty-four times more oxygen is available to the muscles when you are running in the school sports than when you are sitting at a desk.

This is where the cucumber sandwich comes into the story. The sandwich has already been broken down and sent all around the body. Now it meets up with the oxygen in a process called oxidation, which produces heat and energy. (Oxygen seems to like joining up with other elements.) Oxidation can be fast or slow. When it's fast you see a flame. It's often called burning when this happens. When it's very slow, for example when iron and oxygen combine to give rust, you don't see it happening. However it's the same process going on.

As the sandwich "burns" in your body, the heat in it is given off in carefully controlled stages. It has to be slow, otherwise there would be trouble. There's enough heat in a Christmas dinner to kill you if all of it were released into the body at once – in fact, enough to make your blood boil!

You can actually burn your cucumber sandwich in a laboratory experiment to measure the energy (calories) it contains. The sandwich is placed inside what looks like a metal bomb. This is pumped full of oxygen at high pressure and then put into water. Electric wires ignite the sandwich and it burns away in the oxygen,

heating the water at the same time. The increase in water temperature is measured very exactly – this is the heat that was stored in the food, that you would have slowly been given if you'd eaten the sandwich rather than experimented with it.

In your body, the energy from the sandwich burnt in the oxygen is used for only three things – to make you grow, to fuel the body in the same way that petrol fuels a car, and to keep all the various parts of the body in a good state of repair.

18

Beauty's Only Skin Deep

The body of a grown-up has about 75 million million cells in it. This mass of tiny units is covered in skin which is itself made up of cells. Weighing in at about 4 kilograms, the skin is the biggest single organ of your body. It's much bigger than the liver which is the largest internal organ.

Skin clothes the body from head to foot. In some places it is thicker than in others. On the eyelids it's as thin as 0·5 of a millimetre. On the soles of the feet it can be as deep as half a centimetre, or even as much as 1 centimetre in people who walk barefoot all their lives. The average skin thickness over the whole body is 1 to 2 millimetres.

The main job of your skin is to keep you in and other things out. Millions of years ago our ancestors lived in the sea. Now we don't – apart from on our summer holidays – and the world is actually rather a hostile place for a body which is 60 per cent water. So the skin keeps the body water in, and it keeps unwanted water out too – otherwise you would go soggy in the bath.

Skin is like a three-layered cake. On top is the epidermis. In the middle is the dermis, filled with blood vessels, nerve endings, hair roots, and sweat glands. This rests on the lower layer of the cake – a bed of fat. An average square centimetre of skin has 7·5 million cells and contains 200 sweat glands, 30 oil-producing glands, 20 hairs, 1 metre of blood vessels and nearly 4 metres of nerves.

These are only average figures. Skin on the palm of the hands and soles of the feet has no hairs, but a lot more sweat glands (around 460 per square centimetre). You have probably already noticed this. If all the sweat glands in the body were stretched out and laid end to end they would be approximately the length of a marathon race, or about 42 kilometres.

The different parts that go to make up skin all give clues about what else skin does in addition to keeping water in and out. The oil helps to make the skin a barrier to protect your body from germs. The nerves, for which the skin is a base, receive and pass messages to your brain. These register heat, cold, light touch, deep touch (or pressure) and pain. (Most of life's many different sensations are a mixture of these nerve endings jangling. A good firm kiss, you might like to know, is a combination of heat and pressure! A peck on the cheek is mainly light touch with a little heat.)

The tiny blood vessels of the skin are part of your body's temperature control system – when you are hot, blood is moved to your outermost layer so that heat is given off into the air. The sweat glands help you stay cool, too, as sweat evaporates into the air drawing heat with it. When it's cold, your body saves heat by moving blood into your warm innermost parts.

This is why your skin goes white in the cold. The hairs also come into play when it's cold, as they stand on end, trapping a layer of air and acting like a duvet.

So how does the cucumber sandwich fit into all this? It arrives at the skin in the small blood vessels of the dermis. Unless it is needed for immediate energy, the fat in the sandwich is stored in the skin's bed of fat. This layer forms a big fatty blanket which helps keep heat in the body. Some water from the sandwich, with a mixture of dissolved salts, goes to produce sweat.

The sandwich is also vital to the day-to-day turnover of the cells of the skin. There is actually a fourth level of skin. Between the epidermis and the dermis, like jam spread thinly in the cake, is a layer of cells which is continually making cells for the epidermis above.

As the new cells are formed – mainly at night – they move out to the next layer, to replace cells which are being worn or washed away. From the time a cell is formed to the time it is lost is about fifty days. So about every seven weeks your body gets a completely new outer skin.

Not only the skin but most of the body is continually being rebuilt or replaced thanks to food like our sandwich. (While you read that last sentence about 50 million body cells died and were exchanged!) Different parts of the body renew their cells at different rates. Red blood cells last about 120 days before they die and new ones take over. (That means two million are made every second!) In the intestines the cells in contact with the food are worn away in a week. Bone cells may last twenty years. Some parts of the body never make new cells. The brain, for example, is made up of about 14 thousand million cells, but once fully formed that's it – you can't grow more cells. In fact you start off with plenty, and even though the number reduces as you get older you will still have enough.

Until you are about eighteen you are growing, and energy from the sandwich has to produce extra new cells as well as replacing old ones. Cells are the basic building blocks of the body. They are different shapes and sizes depending on what job they have to do, but a typical one is like a small city. There is a wall (or membrane) around the cell, and a central nucleus, a sort of headquarters where the codes and instructions for everything about the body are kept. Then there are some store houses, and also some power stations (called "mitochondria") where energy is produced in a form that the body can use.

To get from one cell, which is how everyone starts, to 75 million million cells by the time you are a grown-up, something remarkable has to go on. (It's called growing up!) What basically happens as you grow is that cells split into two. There isn't much more to it than that. Except that the body has to know when to stop. One interesting fact about animal cells is that they are all more or less the same size. So the individual cells of an elephant's body are much the same size as ours. There are just more of them – 6,500 million million to be exact!

There are lots of ways of imagining all the different cells of the body. They have been compared to the snowflakes that make up a snowman. This is quite a good comparison except that it gives the impression that the cells are all much the same. And they are not. A muscle cell looks different under the microscope from a bone cell, and a skin cell from a brain cell. Each has its own job to do.

But finally let's get back to skin for an unusual thought about cells. Every day millions of cells are either washed away or rubbed off, and these outer layers of skin – the layers that you are touching this book with – are actually dead. So the next time you have to kiss someone you don't like, remember you are only kissing dead tissue. And so are they.

19

Food for Thought

Your brain is a remarkable 1·3 kilogram soft grey-white computer. Though it's easy to describe it as this, the brain is in fact far more powerful than any electronic gadgetry that's ever been made, even though it's 80 per cent water. One scientist has worked out that even the most sophisticated of modern computers still only has the intelligence of a beetle.

The brain is what first thinks of eating the sandwich, and it monitors the process of taking it into the body. It has two control centres set deep inside itself which are concerned with eating. One sends out orders to eat, when the body needs more food – usually when the stomach is empty – and the other orders the body to stop eating when it's had enough. (You can end up eating too much if this second centre goes wrong.)

Messages about the sandwich arrive at the brain through the five senses of the body. You can *see* it. You can *smell* it. You can *touch* it. You can even *hear* your mum telling you it's nearly ready. And when you *taste* it, that's when things really get moving. The stomach starts to prepare itself, and saliva streams into the mouth ready to break down the sandwich. This action of mouth-watering even before the sandwich arrives is the start of digestion.

But where does this computer of a brain gets its energy from? Unlike most other parts of the body the brain can't store energy within itself. So it needs a continual supply of sugar and oxygen delivered. Both these come in blood. This is the reason that the brain – unlike other parts of the body – can only go without blood for about two minutes before it is damaged.

The heart pumps about 5 litres of blood every

minute when the body is at rest, and around 15 per cent of this – 750 millilitres – is sent to the brain. The brain takes more oxygen out of this blood than does any other part of the body. It uses 20 per cent of all the oxygen you breathe in through the lungs. The energy is produced when the sugar from the cucumber sandwich is burnt in oxygen.

But this still does not fully answer the question about where the brain gets its energy. To find out you must look for where the cucumber gets its sugar.

Green plants such as our cucumber make sugar using the sun's energy – this is something *only* green plants can do. The substance in them that gives them their colour – chlorophyll – manufactures sugar out of water and carbon dioxide when the sun's light falls on the leaves. The water comes from the ground through the roots and the carbon dioxide is taken in from the air by the leaves. If an animal – such as you or me – eats the plant, its body can reverse the process by which the plant produced the sugar. The body burns the sugar in oxygen and this gives off the energy that the plant took in from the sun to make the sugar (and it gives off the carbon dioxide and the water that the plant also used).

So the brain gets its energy – the energy contained in the sugar – from solar power! It's not as obvious a link as absorbing the sun's energy directly through the top of your head, but indirectly the sun certainly powers the computer inside your skull.

All this follows a basic rule of life. Although the word "make" is used a lot when talking about energy it is not really the correct word. No one, or no thing for that matter, can actually make energy – or destroy it either. Energy can only be transformed or changed. In this case the plant plays the middle role between changing the light energy of the sun into the energy that works the brain, which is a combination of mostly chemical and a little electrical energy.

You can have some fun with all these facts. The brain needs 80 grams of sugar a day to run. on. This is the same amount of energy as a 10-watt light bulb (rather a dim light bulb – the one in a child's night-light is usually about 15 watts). Glucose is the type of sugar that supplies the brain, and this just happens to be the type of sugar in cucumbers.

What if the brain were only powered by cucumbers? An average cucumber has 9 grams of glucose in it – and not much else except water. (Cucumbers haven't got any fat, for example, and this makes the maths much simpler.) So you divide the 80 grams needed by the 9 grams and you get the number 8·9. Therefore if it only had cucumbers to rely on, your brain would need 8·9 cucumbers per day to work!

20

Water Water Everywhere

Water is probably the most important part of any diet. It's been worked out that you'll drink about 40,000 litres of fluid in a lifetime. You can live for quite a long time without food – about thirty days, depending on how fat you are – but only for a few days without water.

Every day the average person takes in around 2 or 3 litres. Some comes in drinks, but there's a lot in food as well. (Even dry biscuits contain water.) Most foods have more water in them than you would think. The sandwich's bread is 40 per cent water, for example, and the cucumber itself is nearly all water.

There has to be a careful balance between the water coming into the body, and the water going out. If this goes wrong you can either dry out like crispbread, or become waterlogged like a boiled marrow. (If you've ever seen a boiled marrow you'll know what I mean.) Normally the brain keeps a very good control over this balance. If you get dry it makes you feel thirsty. If you drink a lot of water the body gets rid of what you don't need.

In fact the body is losing water in various ways all the time. The most obvious way out is through the two kidneys. These are the washing machines of the body, continually filtering the blood. What they remove is the liquid called urine, and this is passed down two tubes to an elastic muscular bag called the bladder. Here it is stored until you go to the toilet.

89

Urine contains waste material which the body needs to get rid of. If urine production stops for any reason these poisonous wastes build up. About 1800 litres of blood are pumped to the two kidneys by the heart each day. Over a million small tubes in the kidneys filter this and make 1.5 litres of urine out of it. It is fortunate that about 99 per cent of water is returned back into the blood after being filtered – otherwise you'd spend all day in the toilet, drinking furiously to keep pace with what was being lost in the urine!

Every day at least 300 millilitres of urine must be passed to carry the waste away. However this is the absolute minimum. Most of us pass the average 1·5 litres. If you live to be seventy that's 38,325 litres – or 114,975 cucumbers! Seventeen million litres of liquid a second flow over the Boyoma Falls in Zaire – in other words, what it takes the world's greatest waterfall just one second to pass would take 444 people a lifetime!

Passing urine down the toilet isn't the only outlet for water. Quite a lot is lost in sweat from the skin. If you exercise on a hot day in summer you can easily lose a litre of sweat (three cucumbers' worth) in an hour.

Another way out of the body is via the lungs. In the course of a day, nearly half a litre is lost in air breathed out.

Other routes are not quite so important to the body when it comes to getting the balance of water right. But about 200 millilitres (half a cucumber) go every time you open your bowels, and crying loses some, too. However, since this only loses a thin slice of cucumber's worth, this isn't going to dry out even the world's biggest cry baby.

21

The World Constipation Record

There is some doubt about exactly what this record is! One book of "amazing facts" says it is 102 days. A particularly sad case which seems to beat this was of poor Emily Plumley. She was born on 11 June 1850 with no hole in her bottom. These days this could be repaired by surgery, but the operation was not possible then, and the unfortunate Emily lived for 122 days.

Anyway what's left of the cucumber sandwich is likely to move a bit quicker than this. The colon, or large intestine, is the final pathway for undigested food. It's about 1·7 metres long and runs from its junction with the small intestine down to the hole in the bottom, called the anus.

The remains of the sandwich will have arrived at the beginning of the colon about four hours after being eaten. There's an hour or so's hold-up at the junction of the large and small intestine – almost like a customs hold-up at a border between two countries. The sandwich then moves slowly on along the colon up to quite near where the liver is, on the right-hand side under the lower part of the rib cage – this 15-centimetre journey takes another hour. It then turns right in the colon, and moves *very* slowly across to the left side of the body under the rib cage. Here it's quite close to the stomach where it was some nine hours ago.

The next part of its travels in the colon take it down the left side of the body towards the anus, and it eventually arrives here about eighteen hours after the original meal.

During the time in the colon quite a lot of water is taken out of the "food" and absorbed back into the body. When it arrives in the very last part of the bowels – the rectum – it is fairly solid. Most of what is left hasn't come from the sandwich at all, but from bacteria which live in the colon and have literally passed away!

As the rectum fills up, the body feels the need to empty it. Babies have no control over this. When a baby's rectum fills up, its muscles relax and the bowel empties automatically. During the first few years of life the circular muscles around the bottom come under voluntary control, and then you can have a say in when it is convenient to go to the toilet!

Many people have a fascination with their bowels, and worry a great deal about how often they "go". Most have nothing wrong with them – except a rather high expectation of how many times a week they should go to the toilet. Usually they feel they are rather "sluggish", and think they should have a "good clear out" every day.

These sorts of worries get handed down from parents to children, generation after generation. The Victorians were particularly bad about having a toilet obsession. Many of them would try and force their children to go to the toilet – often in cold and hurried conditions with little privacy – and this would slowly lead to the dreaded "sluggish" bowels.

Strong laxatives – often called purgatives – were then used to force the bowel to work. These actually give you "the runs" at first, but after a while the bowel becomes addicted to them and then can't "go" without.

There should be no need for laxatives. The best way to keep your insides working smoothly and trouble free is to eat plenty of fibre. This is mainly cellulose, the carbohydrate material that keeps plants rigid and plant-shaped in the same way that bones give you your shape. You cannot digest this fibre, and it moves through the bowels giving your insides something to grip on to. There should be no need to strain on the toilet after eating the cucumber sandwich and the rest of the food on Christmas Day, as it all contained plenty of fibre. (Foods high in fibre are brown rice, wholemeal bread and pasta, high-fibre breakfast cereals, and fruit and vegetables – including that brussels sprout!)

But back to the world record for constipation. In 1611 a case lasting five months was recorded. Then there are reports in medical books of a man who went from 18 June 1900 to 21 June 1901 without going to the toilet. (This is 368 days if you're trying to work it out in your head.) And there are still more contenders for the title. In 1810 a Paris medical journal mentioned, in passing, someone who had gone – or rather not gone – for two years, and finally a French journal of 1745 would seem to have the record – if you can believe this, and I don't! – at seven years between bowel movements.

The important thing is not to worry about joining these odd record holders. The body is very good at working naturally, and doesn't need worry, or laxatives.

Flower Power

When I was at school the local sewage farm was in the field at the back of the sports field. In the heat of the summer I could see the biggest reddest tomatoes and the most enormous cucumbers growing on the sludge that came out of this place. And if you could get them, these tomatoes and cucumbers that grew courtesy of the village's toilets were the finest imaginable. This had me puzzled at the time. How could such good food grow on material like this?

The answer was that this sludge had everything that was necessary for the plants to grow tall and strong. They could recycle all that was in the muck, using the power of the sun to build these ingredients into fruit which was safe and good to eat.

This shows a basic difference between animals and plants. Plants do not depend on us for food – they can take the sun's energy and save it within themselves. We can't do this. All animals have to rely – either directly or indirectly – on plants for energy. Even when animals eat other animals the chain always goes back to plants and the sun. If you eat beef, the energy in that beef has been built into the cow when it ate the green grass that grew in the sun.

So all the energy we get from food comes to the earth from the sun, either through plants in the soil or plants in the sea. This is a pretty good reason for looking after the world . . . and for having a cucumber sandwich!